DINOSAURS RULE

The incredible
story of
life on Earth

203 to 145 million years ago

Thanks to the creative team:
Senior Editor: Alice Peebles
Designer: Lauren Woods and collaborate agency
Consultant: Paolo Viscardi

First American edition published in 2015 by Lerner Publishing Group, Inc.

First published in Great Britain in 2015 by Hungry Tomato Ltd.

Hungry Tomato™
A division of Lerner Publishing Group, Inc.
241 First Avenue North
Minneapolis, MN 55401 USA

For reading levels and more information, look up this title at www.lernerbooks.com.

Main body text set in Burbank Big Regular Medium.
Typeface provided by House Industries.

Library of Congress Cataloging-in-Publication Data

Rake, Matthew, author.
    Dinosaurs rule / by Matthew Rake.
        pages cm. – (Field guide to evolution)
        Summary: "About 250 million years ago, the first dinosaurs began to roam Earth. Join your friendly prehistoric fish-guide on an adventure through the Triassic and Jurassic eras–thrilling chapters in the story of evolution"– Provided by publisher.
        Audience: Ages 8-12.
        Audience: Grades 4 to 6.
        ISBN 978-1-4677-6349-3 (lb : alk. paper) – ISBN 978-1-4677-7195-5 (pb : alk. paper) – ISBN 978-1-4677-7196-2 (eb pdf)
        1. Dinosaurs–Juvenile literature. I. Title.
QE861.5.R35 2015
567.9–dc23   2014046759

Manufactured in the United States of America
1 - VP - 7/15/15

DINOSAURS RULE

By Matthew Rake

Illustrated by Peter Minister

HUNGRY TOMATO™

MINNEAPOLIS

Everything alive
today is related to
life from the past.

CONTENTS

*mya *means "million years ago"*

Hi, my name is Ackerley. I'm an Acanthostega.

I'm your guide. I've got the world's greatest story to tell you: how life evolved on Earth. Or to put it another way...

...how we all got here.

This is the second book in the series. In the first, **The Dawn of Planet Earth**, we found out how tiny organisms, so small you would need a microscope to see them, evolved into huge reptiles, some the size of elephants.

In this book, I'm going to take you to the Triassic and Jurassic periods, when these reptiles evolved into an amazing variety of creatures.

Some reptiles, known as pterosaurs, developed wings and later became aerial assassins. Except for insects, the pterosaurs were the first animals ever to fly in the skies.

How do we know this stuff?

Scientists who study the history of living things are known as paleontologists. To learn about life in the past, they find and study fossils. Fossils are simply the remains of animals and plants that have been preserved in rocks.

There are two types of fossil: body fossils and trace fossils. A body fossil preserves the actual parts of an animal or plant. A trace fossil preserves the marks that organisms have made. For example, an animal may have made a burrow or footprints, or a plant may have left holes where its roots once were.

Other reptiles moved into the oceans and became ferocious sea monsters, like Liopleurodon. You wouldn't want to mess with this monster. It had **bigger jaws than T. rex's** and would eat just about anything that crossed its path.

Of course, some reptiles stayed on dry land. Many developed into dinosaurs, some as big as double-decker buses...

...some even bigger!

So on land, in the sea, and in the air, the Triassic and Jurassic worlds were full of ruthless predators, all looking for their next meal. But don't worry. We will also meet some of the gentler creatures, such as the huge sauropods who spent all day doing nothing more ferocious than eating leaves.

Changing Shape of the Planet

You may think the map of the world has always looked the same. But the continents have changed dramatically throughout the history of Earth, just as animals and plants have.

About 225 million years ago, the whole world was one big supercontinent called Pangea.

About – 225 million years ago

About 200 million years ago, the continent of Pangea was dividing into Laurasia in the north and Gondwanaland in the south.

About – 200 million years ago

By 65 million years ago, when the dinosaurs were wiped out, the world was looking much more like it does today. Laurasia was splitting up into North America in the west and Europe and Asia in the east. Gondwanaland had split into South America, Africa, India, and Antarctica/Australia.

About – 65 million years ago

In the last 65 million years, North and South America have joined up, Antarctica and Australia separated, and India merged with the continent of Asia.

EVOLUTION TIMELINE

The story begins with the Big Bang 15,000 million years ago (mya). Life on Earth starts around 3,800 mya. Oxygen forms in the atmosphere about 2,300 mya as a waste product of photosynthesizing bacteria, in what the scientists call the Great Oxygenation Event. The ozone layer begins forming in Earth's atmopshere 600 mya. This will protect Earth from the harmful rays of the sun. These events mean that animals will eventually be able to live on the land.

The first reptiles evolve from one branch of amphibians. Reptiles are the first animals with backbones to live permanently on land. Vast forests cover the land, and these will eventually fossilize to become coal.

Sea animals start appearing in the "Cambrian explosion of life" 540 - 520 mya. They swim, crawl, burrow, hunt, defend themselves, and hide away. Some creatures evolve hard parts such as shells.

Life begins on land, as plants grow by lakes, streams, and coasts, and arthropods (animals with segmented bodies, like millipedes) venture onto land. The first jawed fish appear.

Precambrian

Cambrian

Devonian

Carboniferous

Precambrian 4,540-541 mya	Cambrian 541-485 mya	Ordovician 485-443 mya	Silurian 443-419 mya	Devonian 419-359 mya	Carboniferous 359-299 mya

The "golden age of the dinosaurs" witnesses huge herbivore dinosaurs feeding on lush ferns and palm-like cycads. Smaller but vicious meat-eating dinosaurs hunt the great herbivores.

Homo sapiens appear in Africa around 200,000 years ago. By 40,000 years ago, they are also living in Europe, southern Asia, and Australia. Around 16,000 years ago, they move into North America.

Dinosaurs appear, as do the first mammals and the first flying animals with backbones, the pterosaurs.

Many different mammals evolve. Some stay on land. Some, like whales, go back into the water. Some, like monkeys, take to the trees.

Triassic

Jurassic

Cretaceous

Paleogene

Neogene

Quaternary

| Permian 299-252 mya | Triassic 252-201 mya | Jurassic 201-145 mya | Cretaceous 145-66 mya | Paleogene 66-23 mya | Neogene 23-2.6 mya | Quaternary 2.6 mya - now |

SAVAGES IN THE SEA

When **ichthyosaurs** were around, squid and fish needed to make themselves scarce. These ferocious sea monsters had huge eyes for spotting their prey and solid ear bones to hear the vibrations they made. So no matter how gloomy the waters, ichthyosaurs would always find their next meal.

What's more, thanks to their streamlined bodies, they could chase their prey at speeds up to an estimated 25mph (40 kmph). No wonder ichthyosaurs were the top sea predators in the late Triassic and early Jurassic periods.

If you think an ichthyosaur looks like a dolphin, you're right. And it's probably no coincidence. Ichthyosaurs evolved from land reptiles that returned to the water. Their legs developed into fins that made them better swimmers. Around 200 million years later, dolphins did the same thing, evolving from land mammals that returned to the water.

The other creature here is Tanystropheus. It certainly doesn't look like a dolphin... more like a sauropod! Check out that neck...

It's 10 feet (3 meters) long!

Tanystropheus

Tanystropheus doesn't look quite so suited to life in the water. Its neck and tail made up three quarters of its total length. In fact, some scientists think it spent most of its time on land, perched on rocks along the shoreline, snatching fish from the shallows, a bit like fishing with your neck instead of a rod!

ichthyosaur

Precambrian 4,540-541 mya
Cambrian 541-485 mya
Ordovician 485-443 mya
Silurian 443-419 mya
Devonian 419-359 mya
Carboniferous 359-299 mya
Permian 299-252 mya
Triassic 252-201 mya
Jurassic 201-145 mya
Cretaceous 145-66 mya
Paleogene 66-23 mya
Neogene 23-2.6 mya
Quaternary 2.6 mya - present

The first ichthyosaur skeleton was found in 1811 by 12-year-old Mary Anning on the cliffs of Dorset, England. With her dog Tray, she had gone looking for fossils after a period of storms. In 1823, she discovered the first complete skeleton of a plesiosaur, the reptile that took over from the ichthyosaurs as the top sea predator.

Did You Know?

Ichthyosaurs had huge eyes. The Temnodontosaurus species had the biggest, up to 10.5 inches (26 cm) in diameter. That's bigger than a human skull! For comparison, a blue whale's eye is 6 inches (15 cm) in diameter.

11

TINY TERRORS

The first dinosaurs appeared 230 million years ago. But they weren't huge monsters...

more like chicken-sized T. rexes.

Eoraptor here is about 39 inches (1 m) long, including the tail. That's about half my size. Mind you, I wouldn't have gone anywhere near it. Just look at those vicious claws on three of its five fingers, plus it had needle-sharp teeth.

The first dinosaurs were known as theropods, meaning "beast foot" in Greek. They walked on their back legs, with their heads held out in front and their long tails used for balance. This meant they were quick and nimble, such as **Eoraptor**. That was useful for catching tiny animals.

Eoraptors lived at the same time as the **dicynodonts**, a group of herbivorous reptiles that thrived in the Triassic period. They were built like tanks. Some were as big as oxen, some as small as rats. Maybe Eoraptor would have tried its luck with a rat-sized dicynodont.

Eoraptor

What Makes a Theropod?

● Theropod teeth were sharp, curved backward, and serrated like steak knives, perfect for trapping and munching through prey.

● The legs of theropod dinosaurs extended down from the body, unlike reptiles's legs, which usually grew out at the side. Vertical limbs can support a greater weight than sprawling limbs. This helped dinosaurs to grow so large.

● Theropods walked on two legs. They had three main fingers on their hands, usually with sharp claws. The fourth and fifth digits were much smaller.

Dicynodont

EORAPTOR
Location: South America
Length: 39 inches (1 m)

Precambrian	4,540-541 mya
Cambrian	541-485 mya
Ordovician	485-443 mya
Silurian	443-419 mya
Devonian	419-359 mya
Carboniferous	359-299 mya
Permian	299-252 mya
Triassic	**252-201 mya**
Jurassic	201-145 mya
Cretaceous	145-66 mya
Paleogene	66-23 mya
Neogene	23-2.6 mya
Quaternary	2.6 mya - present

Did You Know?

During the middle Triassic period, rauisuchians (raw-i-sook-key-ans) were the top predators. They were not dinosaurs, but reptiles closely related to crocodiles. The largest were about 23 feet (7 m) long.

Eudimorphodon, a type of pterosaur, wasn't a bird or a bat, but a reptile that evolved a layer of skin and muscle stretching from the fourth finger of each arm down to its ankle. It must have been like having a tough cape attached to your body! By flapping its arms, Eudimorphodon could lift itself off the ground.

Why did they need to fly?

Well, it allowed them to escape predators and find new habitats for nesting. It would have also helped them to catch new types of prey, such as flying insects.

The pterosaurs of the sky lasted as long as the dinosaurs on land, from around 230 million years ago until 65 million years ago, when an asteroid hit Earth. And just like the dinosaurs, the pterosaurs got bigger and bigger during this time. The first pterosaurs were the size of paper planes, but by the end of the Cretaceous period some were as massive as fighter jets!

As the pterosaurs grew larger, they also got better at flying. Their arms became longer and their wings more bladelike and aerodynamic. They had one problem, though: as they grew bigger, they needed stronger limbs to get off the ground. Thicker bones would have helped, but those also would have been too heavy. The answer? Hollow bones, with walls no thicker than a playing card and struts inside the bones to add support. Many animals, including dinosaurs, had some hollow bones. However, pterosaurs had many throughout their bodies, not just in the arms but in the pelvis, ribs, and vertebrae.

The first pterosaur fossil was found in 1784 in Bavaria, Germany by the Italian naturalist Cosimo Alessandro Collini. Unfortunately, Collini made one big mistake when he studied his fossil: he thought he was looking at a sea creature with flippers, not a pterosaur with wings.

Eudimorphodon

Precambrian
4,540-541 mya

Cambrian
541-485 mya

Ordovician
485-443 mya

Silurian
443-419 mya

Devonian
419-359 mya

Carboniferous
359-299 mya

Permian
299-252 mya

Triassic
252-201 mya

Jurassic
201-145 mya

Cretaceous
145-66 mya

Paleogene
66-23 mya

Neogene
23-2.6 mya

Quaternary
2.6 mya - present

Did You Know?

Apart from insects, pterosaurs were the first animals to fly and probably evolved from a small gliding ancestor.

BEATING AROUND THE BUSH

Prosauropods were the first dinosaurs to feed only on vegetation, and they were the first animals tall enough to feed on high vegetation. All herbivores before them had been squat, short-necked animals.

Before you say anything, I know I'm a squat, short-necked animal...

but I ate fish, thank you very much!

Scientists can learn a lot from plant as well as animal fossils. Glossopteris was a tree about 12 feet (3.5 m) high with tongue-shaped leaves. It evolved about 300 million years ago. Its fossils have been found in India, South America, Africa, Australia, and Antarctica. This led Austrian geologist Eduard Suess to realize that all these regions must have been part of the same landmass we now call Pangea (see page 7).

Plateosaurus

Most dinosaurs are known from a handful of fossils, but paleontologists have found over 100 **Plateosaurus** skeletons across Europe. Because many were found in the same places, scientists think Plateosaurus must have roamed in herds. They probably traveled across the dry European landscape of the late Triassic period looking for places with water and plant life.

Plateosaurus could probably rear up on its back legs to graze on high vegetation, such as pine and fir trees and cycads, which had stout trunks with crowns of large, stiff evergreen leaves.

It might have eaten plants at ground level, too, although it would have had to compete with other herbivores for these. There were no flowering plants. Those would not appear until 50 million years later. But there were mosses, ferns, and horsetails, all of which we have today.

PLATEOSAURUS
Location: Europe
Length: 33 feet (up to 10 m)

Precambrian	4,540-541 mya
Cambrian	541-485 mya
Ordovician	485-443 mya
Silurian	443-419 mya
Devonian	419-359 mya
Carboniferous	359-299 mya
Permian	299-252 mya
Triassic	**252-201 mya**
Jurassic	201-145 mya
Cretaceous	145-66 mya
Paleogene	66-23 mya
Neogene	23-2.6 mya
Quaternary	2.6 mya - present

Did You Know?

Among the plants that Plateosaurus might have eaten were lycophytes. They have been around for 410 million years, with some species still growing today. In fact, it is the world's oldest living upright plant. Only plants that lie flat, such as mosses, are older.

MEAT-EATING MONSTERS

Desmatosuchus was a type of reptile known as an aetosaur, which means "eagle lizard." It was called this because its skull resembled a bird's. But attached to its bird-like skull was a pig-like snout and a crocodile-like body. What a crazy mix! Oh, and it was covered in plating like an armadillo. It needed a natural suit of armor and those shoulder spikes to survive an attack.

At the end of the Triassic period, meat-eating dinosaurs became the top predators in North and South America. They grew up to 23 feet (7 m) long and would pounce on their prey with their powerful hind legs before finishing off their victims with their sharp teeth and ripping claws.

Today's victim is a Desmatosuchus.

He might look frightening, especially with those big spikes on his shoulders, but he is actually a big softy. Desmatosuchus had small peg-like teeth, hinting that it probably ate soft plants that it uprooted with its shovel-like snout.

American paleontologist Kenneth Carpenter was born and grew up in Japan in 1949. His favorite film when he was a boy was *Godzilla*, about a great monster that ravaged Tokyo. In 1997 in New Mexico, he found the first skeleton of a fearsome new dinosaur and called it **Gojirasaurus**, combining "Gojira," Japanese for Godzilla, with "saurus," Greek for lizard.

GOJIRASAURUS
Location: North America
Length: 20 feet (6 m)

| Precambrian 4,540-541 mya |
| Cambrian 541-485 mya |
| Ordovician 485-443 mya |
| Silurian 443-419 mya |
| Devonian 419-359 mya |
| Carboniferous 359-299 mya |
| Permian 299-252 mya |
| **Triassic 252-201 mya** |
| Jurassic 201-145 mya |
| Cretaceous 145-66 mya |
| Paleogene 66-23 mya |
| Neogene 23-2.6 mya |
| Quaternary 2.6 mya - present |

Gojirasaurus

Desmatosuchus

At the end of the Triassic period, a mass extinction occurred. Scientists aren't sure what caused it: perhaps volcanic eruptions or an asteroid impact. But it wiped out about 75 percent of the species on Earth and started the breakup of Pangea.

Did You Know?

The full name of the species is *Gojirasaurus quayi*. The word *quayi* comes from Quay County, New Mexico, where Kenneth Carpenter discovered the dinosaur.

BATTLE OF THE BIG BEASTS

Believe it or not, two of the biggest beasts of the late Jurassic period went toe-to-toe in epic fights. We know this because the neck of one **Stegosaurus** fossil shows a U-shaped wound that matches the jaws of an **Allosaurus.** And an Allosaurus fossil has a wound in the tail that matches a Stegosaurus tail spike.

Stegosaurus

Allosaurus

Stegosaurus would've had its work cut out against Allosaurus, the top predator of the time. Some scientists think that when Stegosaurus was under threat, blood rushed to the plates on its back, acting as a warning. If this didn't scare an attacker off, Stegosaurus would've lashed out with its tail. And those spikes could do some damage. They were up to 39 inches (1 m) long.

In 1991, scientists found an almost complete skeleton of an Allosaurus in Wyoming, USA. They called him "Big Al," even though he was six years old when he died and had not quite reached adult size.

Big Al's skeleton shows he suffered 11 broken bones. The first in his tail was caused by a fall, perhaps after being hit by a Stegosaurus tail! He also had broken ribs, probably the result of fighting another Allosaurus.

His final injury, a broken toe, stopped him from getting to water. His skeleton was found with its head and tail pulled up into an arc, a sign that his body dried out in the sun, which suggests there wasn't much water around.

Allosaurus was one big, mean fighting machine.

Its teeth were about 4 inches (10 cm) long, razor sharp, and growing all the time, ready to replace old and lost ones. Some scientists even think Allosaurus attacked with an open mouth, using its jaws like a hatchet to slash into its victim's flesh.

But surely even a creature as savage as Allosaurus wouldn't take on a Stegosaurus? After all, Stegosaurus was built like a tank and had that fearsome spiked tail for protection...

| Precambrian 4,540-541 mya |
| Cambrian 541-485 mya |
| Ordovician 485-443 mya |
| Silurian 443-419 mya |
| Devonian 419-359 mya |
| Carboniferous 359-299 mya |
| Permian 299-252 mya |
| Triassic 252-201 mya |
| **Jurassic 201-145 mya** |
| Cretaceous 145-66 mya |
| Paleogene 66-23 mya |
| Neogene 23-2.6 mya |
| Quaternary 2.6 mya - present |

Did You Know?

The spiked tail of Stegosaurs is known as a thagomizer. This name was coined as a joke in 1982 by cartoonist Gary Larson in his comic strip *The Far Side*, but soon the word was also being used by scientists.

GENTLE GIANTS

Hey, if you think elephants are huge, you should check out the sauropods. They were massive plant-eating dinosaurs that probably evolved from a prosauropod ancestor in the middle of the Jurassic period.

To me, they look like walking whales.

They had big bodies with ridiculously long necks and tails, but their heads were tiny with small brains. They were still clever enough, though, to survive in their environment.

Scientists used to think sauropods, such as **Diplodocus**, evolved their long necks to reach the highest leaves in the trees. This idea makes perfect sense. Like today's giraffes, they would have had their own private food source, out of reach of all the herbivorous animals at ground level, and been able to spot sources of food or threats from predators from a distance.

However, there is a problem. How did their hearts pump blood to heights of over 33 feet (10 m)? One expert estimated that their hearts would have had to weigh 1.6 tons (1,450 kg)! So he suggested that sauropods had extra hearts in their necks to help the pumping.

Diplodocus

DIPLODOCUS
Location: North America
Length: 98.5 feet (about 30 m)

This theory is not quite as silly as it seems. Some animals, such as the hagfish, do have more than one heart. The trouble is, no sauropod fossils have been found with extra hearts. Perhaps sauropods held their necks horizontally, so they could reach plants in swamps, rivers, and dense woodland, only raising them to spot predators or to feed high in the trees.

What did sauropods use their tails for? Scientists have been arguing about this for a long time. Some claim that the tail acted as a third leg for rearing up to trees. Others say a sauropod could swing the tip of its tail faster than the speed of sound and snapped it like a whip to create a massive noise that would frighten off predators. However, that would probably have caused Diplodocus permanent injury! The main purpose of the tail seems to have been simply to counterbalance the neck.

| Precambrian 4,540-541 mya |
| Cambrian 541-485 mya |
| Ordovician 485-443 mya |
| Silurian 443-419 mya |
| Devonian 419-359 mya |
| Carboniferous 359-299 mya |
| Permian 299-252 mya |
| Triassic 252-201 mya |

Jurassic 201-145 mya

| Cretaceous 145-66 mya |
| Paleogene 66-23 mya |
| Neogene 23-2.6 mya |
| Quaternary 2.6 mya - present |

Did You Know?

Supersaurus, at 108-112 feet (33-34 m) long, is the longest sauropod known from reasonably complete remains.

RULERS OF THE OCEANS

Liopleurodon was a Pliosaur and the big boss of the Jurassic seas. It was a powerful swimmer, with four strong, paddle-like limbs, and a sleek, streamlined body. Its jaws were 6.5-8 feet (2-2.5 m) longer than even those of T. rex. What's more, it had powerful muscles at the back of its jaws to help drive its teeth into its prey.

Some scientists think Liopleurodon was an ambush predator that could rapidly accelerate to catch its prey. This would have helped it gobble up the hundreds of pounds of food it needed each day to maintain its massive weight.

Liopleurodon - a type of Pliosaur

Liopleurodon certainly wasn't a fussy eater. It had a taste for fish, including small sharks, squid, and even hard-shelled nautiloids. It would also have a go at the long-necked **plesiosaurs**. We know this because the skeleton of a plesiosaur called **Kimmerosaurus** has marks that match a Liopleurodon's teeth.

Kimmerosaurus - a type of Plesiosaur

The Jurassic seas were full of of swimming reptiles...

including two
giant predators –

plesiosaurs and pliosaurs. Their names might sound similar and they were related, but they looked very different. Plesiosaurs were very graceful, while pliosaurs were big bruisers with massive heads and jaws. While plesiosaurs ate fish, pliosaurs gulped down just about anything... including plesiosaurs.

LIOPLEURODON
Location: European Seas
Length: 23 feet (7 m)

| Precambrian 4,540-541 mya |
| Cambrian 541-485 mya |
| Ordovician 485-443 mya |
| Silurian 443-419 mya |
| Devonian 419-359 mya |
| Carboniferous 359-299 mya |
| Permian 299-252 mya |
| Triassic 252-201 mya |

Jurassic 201-145 mya

| Cretaceous 145-66 mya |
| Paleogene 66-23 mya |
| Neogene 23-2.6 mya |
| Quaternary 2.6 mya - present |

In 2006 in the Arctic islands of Svalbard, scientists found a huge pliosaur skeleton. At first, they couldn't tell what it was, because the fossil was in thousands of bits. Putting it together was like doing a gigantic 3D jigsaw puzle. No wonder it took about six years to complete. Eventually, in 2012, they had enough to estimate its length at 33-43 feet (10-13 m). This made it the biggest pliosaur of them all! They called this new find *Pliosaurus funkei.*

Did You Know?
Water flowed in through Liopleurodon's open mouth and out through its nostrils, so it could smell the scent of any prey in the water.

25

WINGING IT

You think all the dinosaurs died out millions and millions of years ago?

Well, that's not quite true.

Descendants of dinosaurs are around today. They are called birds. So next time you see a sparrow or a seagull or even a stork, remember you are looking at a flying dinosaur!

In 1861, a near-complete skeleton of a mysterious animal from 150 million years ago was found in Germany. Named **Archaeopteryx**, it looked like a bird, but with jaws and teeth, as well as wings and feathers. It also looked like a dinosaur. It had a long, bony tail, and three fingers with claws growing from its wings.

Some scientists at the time were convinced the fossil showed that some dinosaurs had evolved into birds. But most thought this theory was way too far-fetched. It was only in 1969, over 100 years later, that scientists took the idea seriously again. They found another bird-like dinosaur called *Deinonychus antirrhopus* in Montana.

Since then, scientists have found fossils of more than 20 feathered dinosaurs, including, in 2008, **Epidexipteryx**. It couldn't fly, but scientists think it lived out of danger in trees, feeding on insects. Virtually all scientists now agree that birds are descended from the dinosaurs.

In 1859, Charles Darwin published *On the Origin of Species*, a book that is still read today. In it, he claimed that animals evolved by natural selection. That means they change gradually over millions of years. For instance, they might develop wings to help them fly or flippers and fins to help them swim. Archaeopteryx, which was discovered two years after Darwin published his book, was evidence of his theory. It showed an animal in the middle of its evolution from dinosaur to bird.

Epidexipteryx

EPIDEXIPTERYX
Location: China
Length: 17.5 inches (44.5 cm)

Precambrian 4,540-541 mya
Cambrian 541-485 mya
Ordovician 485-443 mya
Silurian 443-419 mya
Devonian 419-359 mya
Carboniferous 359-299 mya
Permian 299-252 mya
Triassic 252-201 mya
Jurassic **201-145 mya**
Cretaceous 145-66 mya
Paleogene 66-23 mya
Neogene 23-2.6 mya
Quaternary 2.6 mya - present

Did You Know?

The dinosaurs that had feathers may have developed the ability to fly by gliding out of trees or by taking off by running along the ground.

SMALL BUT DEADLY

Compsognathus looked pretty much like its cousin T. rex. It had the same razor-sharp teeth and claws, upright stance, and powerful back legs for pouncing on its prey.

The big difference was...

Compsognathus, as you can see here, was the size of a chicken, not a double-decker bus!

But, that wouldn't be much consolation to the tiny mammals that scampered around the forest floors of the Jurassic period. They would have been a tasty meal for a Compsognathus, along with the odd side dish of lizard.

Compsognathus

There were lots of mammals living in the age of the dinosaurs, but unfortunately we haven't found many complete fossils of them. More often than not, just their teeth remain!

We do know that mammals stayed out of the way of the ferocious dinosaurs. That's why they were all small. Many hunted at night when it was safer to go out. Some even lived in the trees or underground.

Fruitafassor was probably one of several mammals that burrowed underground. With its pointed snout and long front claws, it could easily dig holes. **Castorocauda**, on the other hand, could simply dive into water to escape dinosaurs. It was a superb swimmer, helped by its flattened tail, which was similar to a modern beaver's. And it had limbs like a modern platypus, good for both swimming and diggiing.

COMPSOGNATHUS
Location: Western Europe
Length: 2 feet (60 cm) long

Precambrian 4,540-541mya	
Cambrian 541-485 mya	
Ordovician 485-443 mya	
Silurian 443-419 mya	
Devonian 419-359 mya	
Carboniferous 359-299 mya	
Permian 299-252 mya	
Triassic 252-201 mya	
Jurassic 201-145 mya	
Cretaceous 145-66 mya	
Paleogene 66-23 mya	
Neogene 23-2.6 mya	
Quaternary 2.6 mya - present	

Scientists used to think **Compsognathus** was the smallest dinosaur. But now most believe there were several smaller types, including **Parvicursor**, which was about 16 inches (40 cm) long, and possibly **Microraptor**, which was about 20 inches (50 cm) long. Microraptor had a long tail, so it's hard to judge its length, and bizarrely, it had four wings on its four limbs for gliding between trees.

Did You Know?
Compsognathus relied on speed to capture prey, with its long tail providing the balance needed during the chase. Once it caught up with the prey, it could snatch it with its three-fingered hands.

Tanystropheus

Pronounced: tan-ee-stroh-fee-us

The reason Tanystropheus evolved such a long neck has puzzled scientists. Some think this creature might have used its neck not to dip into the water to catch fish but to pluck tree-dwelling reptiles from branches.

Dicynodont

Pronounced: die-sin-no-dont

Dicynodonts were therapsids, or mammal-like reptiles. This creature looked like a pig or a hippo, but it had a beak like a turtle's, plus two tusks in its upper jaw, as have walruses. Its name means "*two dog tooth*," a reference to the tusks.

Eudimorphodon

Pronounced: you-die-more-fo-don

The fossils of pterosaurs like Eudimorphodon are very fragile, and few good ones have been found. These have been dicovered mainly in western Europe and in Brazil. Scientists think some teeth found in Texas may have belonged to Eudimorphodon, but they can't be sure, since no other body parts have been found.

Allosaurus

Pronounced: al-oh-sore-us

About 46 Allosauruses have been found in the Cleveland Lloyd Quarry in Utah. Scientists think that both herbivorous and some carnivorous dinosaurs became trapped in the mud, and that the Allosauruses, looking for an easy meal, met the same fate!

Liopleurodon

Pronounced: lie-oh-ploor-oh-don

Liopleourodon was a massive beast, but how big is hard to say. Very few fossils have been found, and some of those thought to be Liopleurodon could actually belong to other animals. Scientists' best estimates are that it was about 23 feet (7 m) long, but could have been as much as 33 feet (10 m). Its weight was around 25 tons (22,300kg).

Diplodocus

Pronounced: dip-low-doe-kuss
For almost 100 years, "Dippy," the Diplodocus skeleton at the Natural History Museum in London, stood with its tail on the ground. In 1993, scientists at the museum realized the tail probably counterbalanced the neck, so it was lifted in the air.

Plateosaurus

Pronounced: plat-ee-oh-sore-us
Adult Plateosauruses came in many different sizes: some reached only 16 feet (4.8 m) in length, while others were 33 feet (10 m). Scientists think this may be because some found areas with lots of plant life, while other weren't so successful!

Stegosaurus

Pronounced: steg-oh-sore-us
Despite being the size of a bus, Stegosaurus had a brain the size of a dog's: not much bigger than a walnut! In the 19th century, the famous paleontologist Othniel Marsh found an empty space near the hip in a Stegosaurus fossil. He thought it must have contained another brain. It actually contained a bundle of nerves.

Desmatosuchus

Pronounced: dez-mat-oh-soo-kuss
Desmatosuchus was a type of aetosaur, some of which are believed to have built nests. In 1996, geologist Stephen Hasiotis discovered fossilized, bowl-like nests in Arizona that were 220 million years old. The nests were very similar to those made by modern-day crocodiles that dig in the sand of a river bank.

Epidexipteryx

Pronounced: ep-ih-dex-ip-teh-rix
Epidexipteryx's body was covered in small feathers, and from its tail it had four long, ribbon-like display feathers. The tail feathers were probably used to attract a mate but might also have helped it balance on branches and ward off predators. Since the discovery of the Epidexipteryx, some scientists think feathers evolved for the purposes of display before they evolved for flight.

INDEX

THE AUTHOR
Matthew Rake lives in London and has worked in publishing for more than 20 years. He has written on a wide variety of topics, including science, sports, and the arts.

THE ARTIST
Peter Minister started out as a special-effects sculptor and had a successful and exciting career producing sculptures and props for museums, theme parks, TV and film. He now works in CGI, which allows him to express himself with a big ball of digital clay in a more creative way than any "real" clay. His CGI dinosaurs and other animals have appeared in numerous books worldwide.